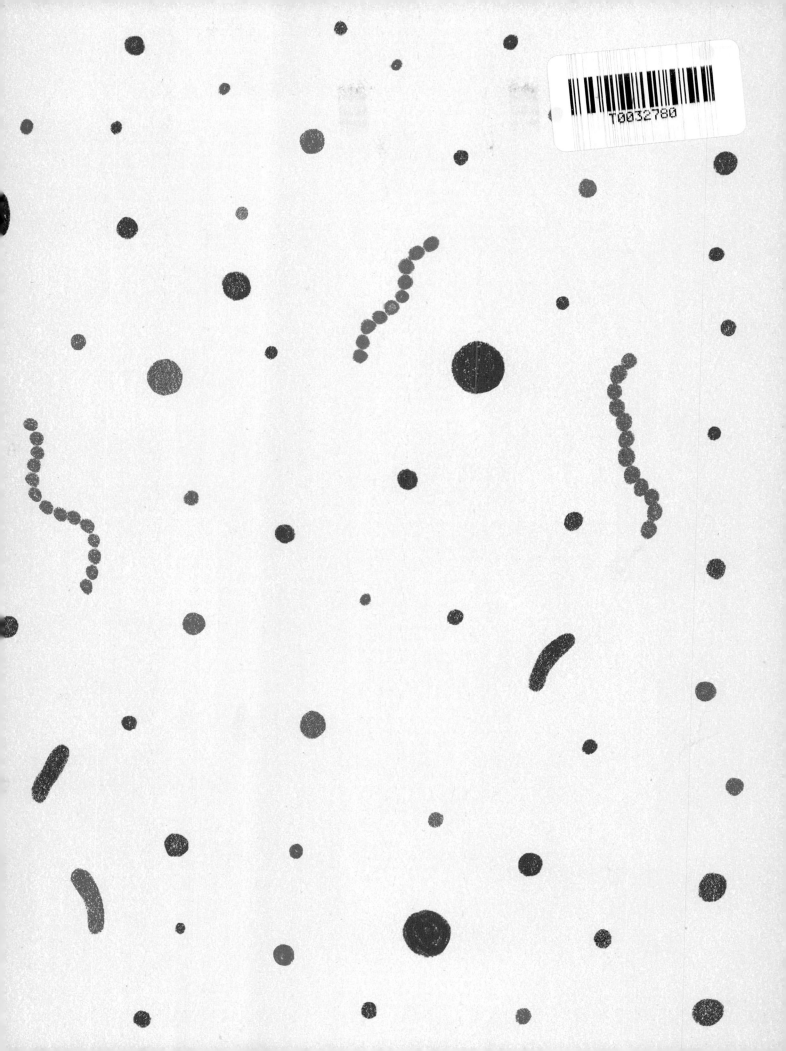

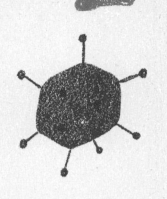

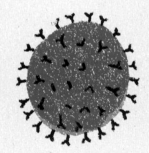

For my colleagues at MGH-Charlestown
HealthCare Center—what an honor to
work with you to care for our patients
and each other
—RL

For Alison—
Always grateful to have you
as my sister!
—KM

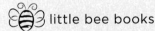 little bee books

New York, NY
Text copyright © 2023 by Rajani LaRocca
Illustrations copyright © 2023 by Kathleen Marcotte
All rights reserved, including the right of reproduction
in whole or in part in any form.
For information about special discounts on bulk purchases,
please contact Little Bee Books at sales@littlebeebooks.com.
Manufactured in China RRD 0323
First Edition
2 4 6 8 10 9 7 5 3 1
ISBN 978-1-4998-1326-5 (hc)
ISBN 978-1-4998-1425-5 (eb)
littlebeebooks.com

 MIX
Paper | Supporting
responsible forestry
FSC® C144853
FSC
www.fsc.org

A Vaccine Is Like a Memory

Newbery Honoree
RAJANI LAROCCA, MD

KATHLEEN MARCOTTE

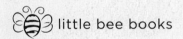
little bee books

Do you remember the last time you were sick?
Maybe you had a sniffly nose or a cough. Maybe
your stomach felt funny. Maybe you had a fever.

Eventually, you felt better.
But do you remember *every* time you've been sick?

Even if you don't, your body remembers.

Infections that make you sick are caused by tiny germs that are too small to see.

These germs spread easily by coughing, sneezing, touching, eating, drinking, or just breathing. They are often mild, but some can cause people to get very sick or even die.

Ahhhh Chooo

With many diseases, you can't get sick from them more than once because your body remembers and destroys the germs before you get sick again.

But what if your body could recognize a disease so you could fight it off without ever having to be sick? Thanks to vaccines, it can!

A vaccine is like a memory
of a disease you never had.

But where did the idea for
vaccines come from?

Before vaccines, people everywhere got very sick and died from all kinds of serious infections.

For hundreds of years, one of the most harmful infections was a disease called **smallpox**. This virus caused high fevers and painful blisters all over the body. People didn't understand what caused smallpox, so they struggled with how to avoid it.

Entire families or villages could be wiped out in **epidemics**, where the disease spread to many people in a community.

But then doctors started to notice that people who had gotten smallpox, and survived, didn't get the disease again.

In the early 1700s, doctors came up with a new idea—which was actually an old idea that had been tried 200 years earlier in China and India—giving people a small, controlled infection with smallpox so they wouldn't get sick when they caught it from other people. This is called **inoculation** and was the precursor to modern-day vaccination.

To inoculate, doctors took a little bit of one person's smallpox sore and injected it into another person who had never had smallpox.

This usually caused a few sores, and sometimes the person got a fever, but it was much less severe than if they had gotten smallpox another way. Inoculated people usually got better and were protected from ever getting smallpox again.

In 1796, an English physician, Edward Jenner, noticed something important. He saw that people who contracted and recovered from a similar but much milder disease, called **cowpox**, also didn't get smallpox.

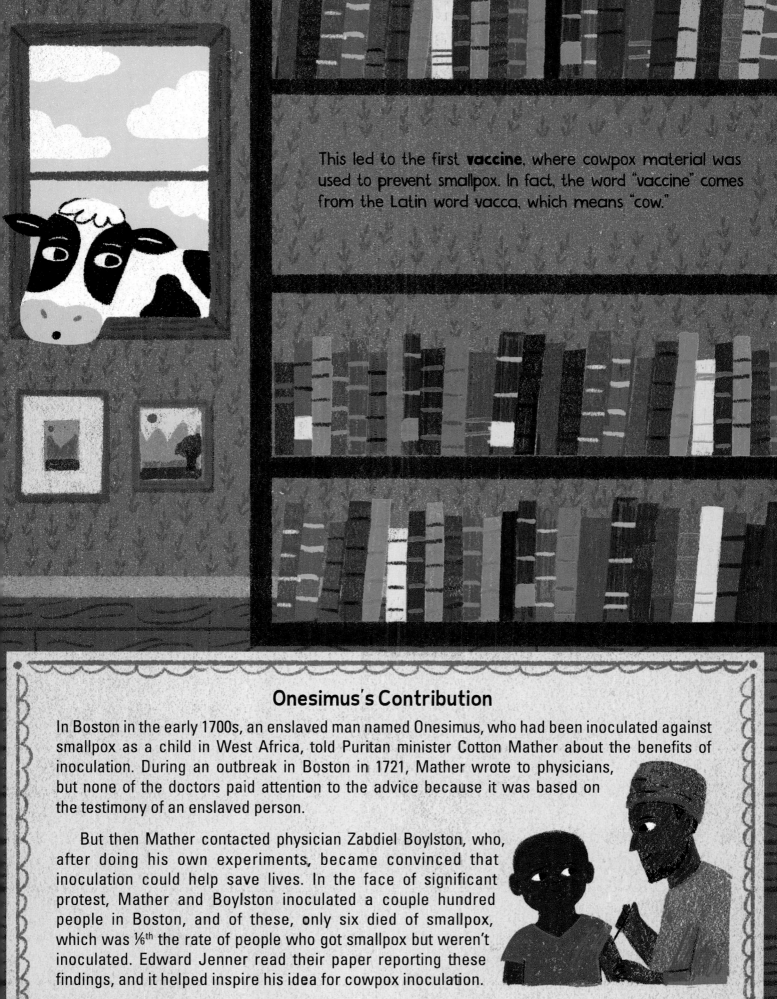

This led to the first **vaccine**, where cowpox material was used to prevent smallpox. In fact, the word "vaccine" comes from the Latin word vacca, which means "cow."

Onesimus's Contribution

In Boston in the early 1700s, an enslaved man named Onesimus, who had been inoculated against smallpox as a child in West Africa, told Puritan minister Cotton Mather about the benefits of inoculation. During an outbreak in Boston in 1721, Mather wrote to physicians, but none of the doctors paid attention to the advice because it was based on the testimony of an enslaved person.

But then Mather contacted physician Zabdiel Boylston, who, after doing his own experiments, became convinced that inoculation could help save lives. In the face of significant protest, Mather and Boylston inoculated a couple hundred people in Boston, and of these, only six died of smallpox, which was ⅙th the rate of people who got smallpox but weren't inoculated. Edward Jenner read their paper reporting these findings, and it helped inspire his idea for cowpox inoculation.

The first National Vaccine Agency in the United States was established in 1813 with the goal of providing the smallpox vaccine to everyone.

Smallpox deaths went down significantly wherever the vaccine was given out.

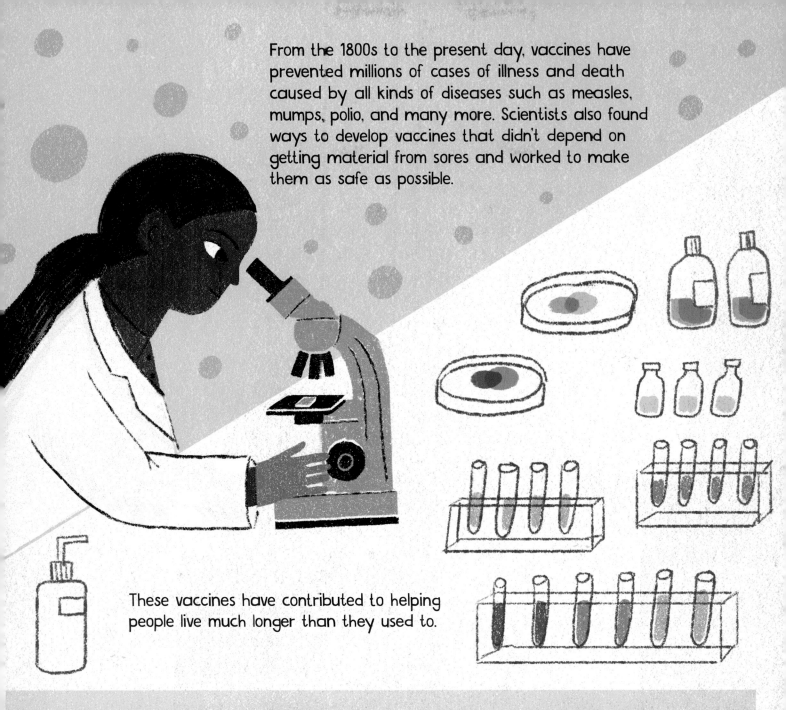

From the 1800s to the present day, vaccines have prevented millions of cases of illness and death caused by all kinds of diseases such as measles, mumps, polio, and many more. Scientists also found ways to develop vaccines that didn't depend on getting material from sores and worked to make them as safe as possible.

These vaccines have contributed to helping people live much longer than they used to.

The 1925 Serum Run to Nome

In the winter of 1925, there was a deadly outbreak of a disease called diphtheria in the town of Nome, Alaska. To save the people from an epidemic, antiserum made from the blood of immunized animals was taken by dogsled relay for 674 miles from Anchorage to Nome. Twenty mushers and 150 sled dogs braved negative tempatures to make the daring run in five days, delivering the antiserum intact and saving the town. Two of the lead dogs, Togo and Balto, became famous across the country! The Iditarod Trail Sled Dog Race runs each year from Anchorage to Nome to commemorate the serum run that saved so many lives.

But how do vaccines actually work?

IMMUNE SYSTEM

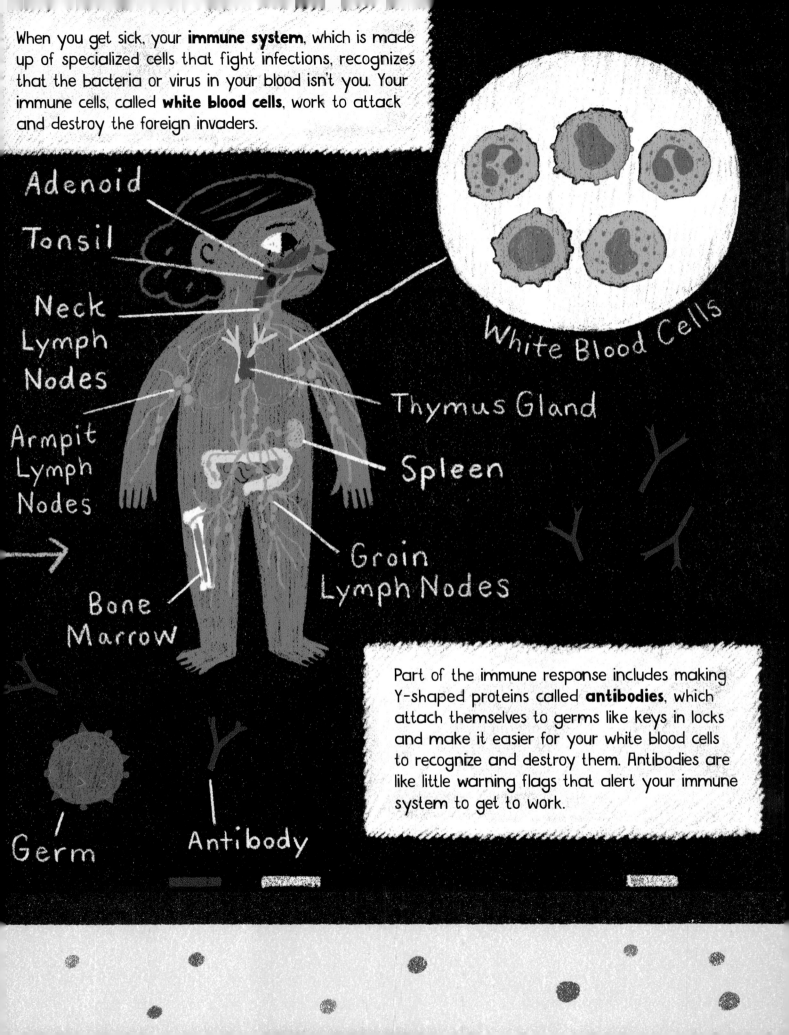

When you get sick, your **immune system**, which is made up of specialized cells that fight infections, recognizes that the bacteria or virus in your blood isn't you. Your immune cells, called **white blood cells**, work to attack and destroy the foreign invaders.

White Blood Cells

Adenoid

Tonsil

Neck Lymph Nodes

Armpit Lymph Nodes

Bone Marrow

Thymus Gland

Spleen

Groin Lymph Nodes

Germ

Antibody

Part of the immune response includes making Y-shaped proteins called **antibodies**, which attach themselves to germs like keys in locks and make it easier for your white blood cells to recognize and destroy them. Antibodies are like little warning flags that alert your immune system to get to work.

From then on, anytime your body encounters those specific germs, it has antibodies ready to remind the immune system that it should destroy the invaders before they make you sick . . . and before you can make anyone else sick.

A vaccine kickstarts your immune system to make antibodies that can fight an infection without actually having to be sick from it. Then, if you're later exposed to that germ, your body "remembers" how to fight it off with these antibodies. Most of the time, it takes more than one dose of a vaccine to make your body produce enough antibodies to protect you.

CHALK

Once enough people have been vaccinated, there are so few people who can spread the disease that everyone is protected—including those who are too young to get the vaccine or who have medical problems that make them unable to get some vaccines. This is called **herd immunity**.

Nowadays, vaccines are made in laboratories and are tested over and over before new ones are approved for use. Because vaccines are used in healthy people to prevent disease, they need to be proven to be both *effective* (good at preventing a disease) and *safe* (not causing bad side effects).

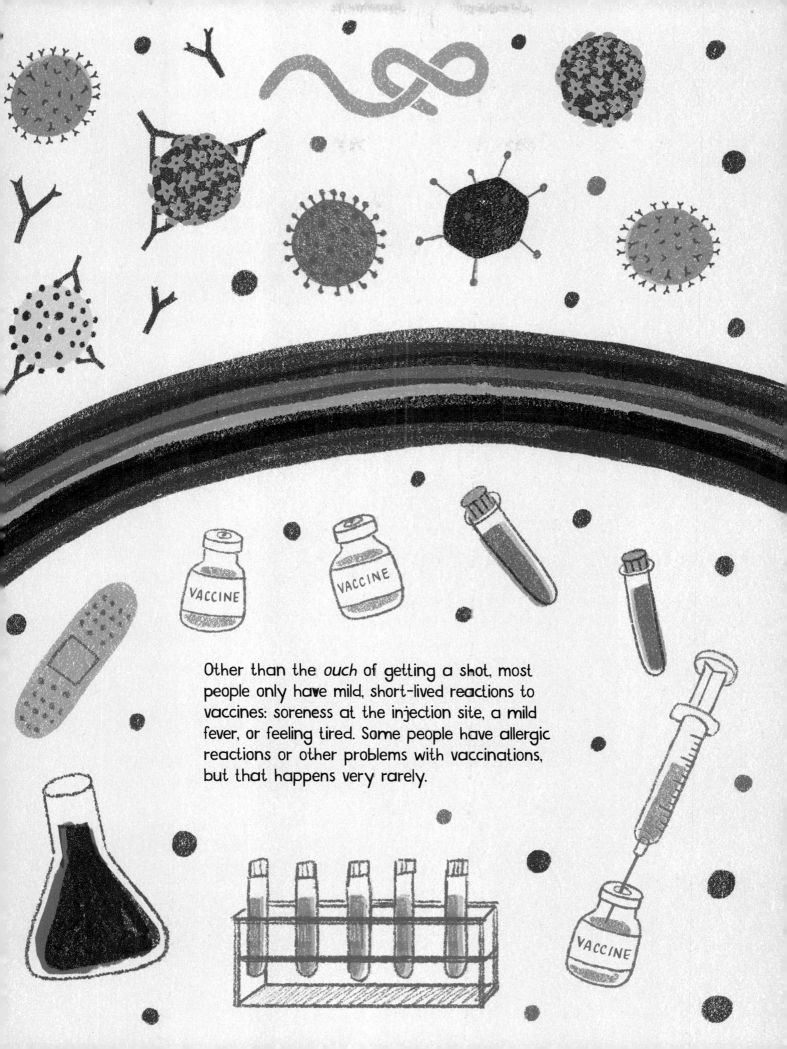

Other than the *ouch* of getting a shot, most people only have mild, short-lived reactions to vaccines: soreness at the injection site, a mild fever, or feeling tired. Some people have allergic reactions or other problems with vaccinations, but that happens very rarely.

In late 2019, a new virus appeared: a coronavirus named SARS-CoV-2, also known as COVID-19. It spread across the world in a **pandemic**, causing millions of infections on every continent and country.

Some people with COVID-19 didn't even realize they were sick. Some had mild symptoms of fever, cough, loss of smell, and diarrhea. And unfortunately, many others got very sick and died.

BREAKING NEWS:
STAY AT HOME!

HAND SANITIZER

Because COVID-19 is very contagious, businesses and schools had to be shut down, and travel was restricted. People were no longer allowed to gather in large groups. Wearing masks in public and washing hands frequently was encouraged. People even had to stop hugging and shaking hands and had to stay away from loved ones and friends.

Scientists raced to make vaccines that could prevent severe illness and stop the spread of this new virus. And in December 2020, faster than any vaccine had ever been developed before, the first COVID-19 vaccines were found to be *safe* and *effective*, and were approved. Some used vaccine technology that had never been used before.

The COVID-19 vaccines helped people's immune systems recognize and eliminate the virus without them having to get sick. They provided a glimmer of hope in a time when so many had been devastated by COVID-19.

Because of the COVID-19 vaccines, schools and businesses were able to open again.

But the virus continued to infect unvaccinated people, and over time it changed, or **mutated**, so that it could infect even vaccinated people. But the vaccines helped prevent severe illness.

Because of vaccines, diseases like polio and smallpox have disappeared entirely. Because of vaccines, most doctors in the U.S. have never seen a case of measles or diphtheria. In countries where vaccines aren't as readily available, many people can die of illnesses that we hardly see anymore in the U.S.

But we can't forget what it was like not too long ago when these diseases were common. And without enough vaccinated people, these dangerous diseases could come back.

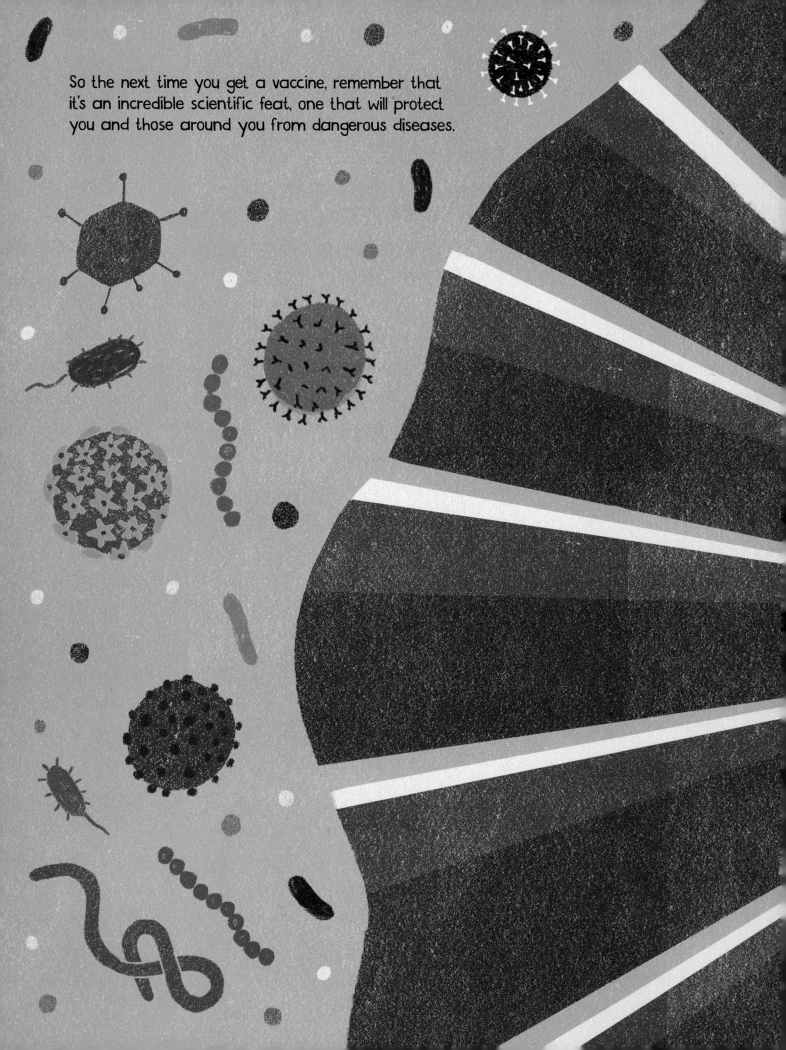

So the next time you get a vaccine, remember that it's an incredible scientific feat, one that will protect you and those around you from dangerous diseases.

Because a vaccine is powerful.
A vaccine is protective.

A vaccine is like a memory of a disease you
never had, so you and others won't get sick!

Types of Germs

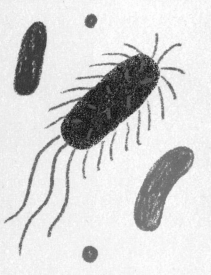

Bacterium (plural: bacteria): a microscopic, single-celled organism that lives in animals, plants, soil, and water. Some bacteria, such as those that live in the human digestive system, are helpful to humans; others can cause diseases.
Examples: E. coli (can cause severe diarrhea, urinary tract infections), Streptococcus (can cause throat infections, skin infections)

Fungus (plural: fungi): a group of complex, spore-producing microorganisms that feed on organic matter, such as molds, yeast, mushrooms, and toadstools. In the body, some fungi can cause diseases. Others are used to develop antibiotics and antitoxins, since they can make products that kill bacteria.
Examples: Candida (causes thrush), Epidermophyton (causes ringworm)

Parasite: an organism that lives on or in a host organism and gets its food from or at the expense of the host.
Examples: Plasmodium falciparum (causes malaria), head lice

Virus: an extremely tiny infectious agent that can live and multiply only inside the living cells of animals, plants, or bacteria.
Examples: Adenovirus (causes the common cold), Varicella (causes chicken pox), Influenza (causes flu), SARS-CoV-2 (causes COVID-19)

Common Infections We Now Have Vaccines For

- **Cholera**, which causes fever and severe diarrhea
- **COVID-19**, which causes a variety of symptoms, including respiratory and gastrointestinal
- **Diphtheria**, which causes a membrane to coat the throat and made people unable to breathe
- **Haemophilus influenzae**, which causes lung and brain infections
- **Influenza**, which causes fever, respiratory symptoms. and pneumonia
- **Measles**, which causes a high fever, rash, and lung infection
- **Meningococcus**, which causes infections around the brain and spinal cord
- **Pertussis**, or "whooping cough," which causes a severe cough and obstruction of the throat
- **Pneumococcus**, which causes lung infections and infections around the brain and spinal cord
- **Polio**, which causes fever and muscle paralysis
- **Rabies**, which causes nerve problems, throat spasms, and death
- **Tetanus**, which causes muscle spasms, paralysis, and death
- **Tuberculosis**, which causes fever, severe cough, and weight loss
- **Typhoid fever**, which causes a high fever, rash, stomach pain, and cough
- **Yellow fever**, which causes fever, fatigue, abdominal pain, and jaundice (a yellow discoloration to the eyes and skin)

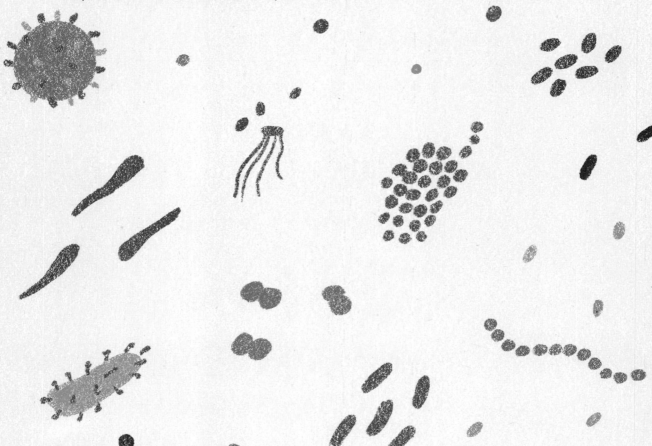

Types of Vaccines

1. Live, Attenuated (weakened) Virus

These vaccines use a small amount of a virus that's been made weak in the laboratory. These vaccines usually result in a strong response from the immune system and antibodies that last for years after vaccination. However, some people with weak immune systems, or who take certain medications, shouldn't get these vaccines because they may make them sick with the disease. Examples of these kinds of vaccines include:

- Measles, Mumps, and Rubella (MMR)
- Chicken pox (Varicella)
- Rotavirus
- Smallpox

2. Inactivated (killed) Virus

These vaccines use a killed version of a virus to stimulate the body's immune response. The immune system doesn't react as strongly to these types of vaccines, so multiple doses and booster (reminder) shots may be needed later. Examples include:

- Influenza
- Hepatitis A
- Polio
- Rabies

3. Subunit Vaccines (vaccines targeting pieces of germs)

These vaccines use specific pieces of a germ, like its protein, sugar, or capsid (casing), to stimulate the immune system. These are safe to use in everyone, including those with weak immune systems. These vaccines typically need booster shots over time.
Examples:

- Pneumococcus
- Meningococcus
- Haemophilus Influenzae Type B (HiB)
- Pertussis (Whooping Cough)
- Hepatitis B
- Human Papillomavirus
- Shingles

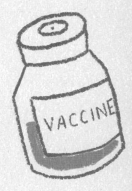

4. Toxoid Vaccines

These vaccines target germs' toxins, or the products that make people sick—not the actual germ—to prevent illness. These vaccines require boosters. Examples:

- Tetanus
- Diphtheria

5. mRNA Vaccines

The first two COVID-19 vaccines were a brand-new type of vaccine, ones that use molecules called Messenger RNA, or mRNA. mRNA is used inside your body's cells when you "translate" the code from your DNA to make proteins. In the lab, scientists created mRNA molecules which "code" for the COVID19 virus's "spike protein." When the mRNA vaccine enters a muscle cell, the cell uses it to make the COVID19 spike protein and put it on the outside of the cell membrane. That makes the body's immune system react to it and form antibodies . . . all without getting the virus itself!

6. Adenovirus Vaccines

These vaccines drop genetic information from the disease they protect against into a different kind of virus—in this case, adenovirus, which causes the common cold—to make your cells produce proteins to stimulate the body's immune response. However, it's important that recipients of this kind of vaccine have never had this type of adenovirus before. That's why, for the COVID-19 adenovirus vaccine, the scientists used a chimpanzee adenovirus, one that has been changed so it can enter human cells, but it can't replicate inside cells and make people sick. The immune response to this type of vaccine can be quite strong, so a single dose can be very effective. Several types of adenovirus vaccines are being studied:

- COVID-19
- HIV
- Tuberculosis
- Ebola
- Malaria

Bibliography:
Centers for Disease and Prevention. "Understanding mRNA COVID-19 Vaccines." Accessed September 2021.
https://www.cdc.gov/coronavirus/2019-ncov/vaccines/different-vaccines/mRNA.html
Max Kozlov, "Introducing Inoculation, 1721," *The Scientist* online, (January 1, 2021). Accessed June 2022.
https://www.the-scientist.com/foundations/introducing-inoculation-1721-68275
The College of Physicians of Philadelphia. "The History of Vaccines." Accessed September 2021.
https://www.historyofvaccines.org/timeline
U.S. Department of Health & Human Services. "Vaccine Safety." Accessed September 2021.
https://www.hhs.gov/immunization/basics/safety/index.html

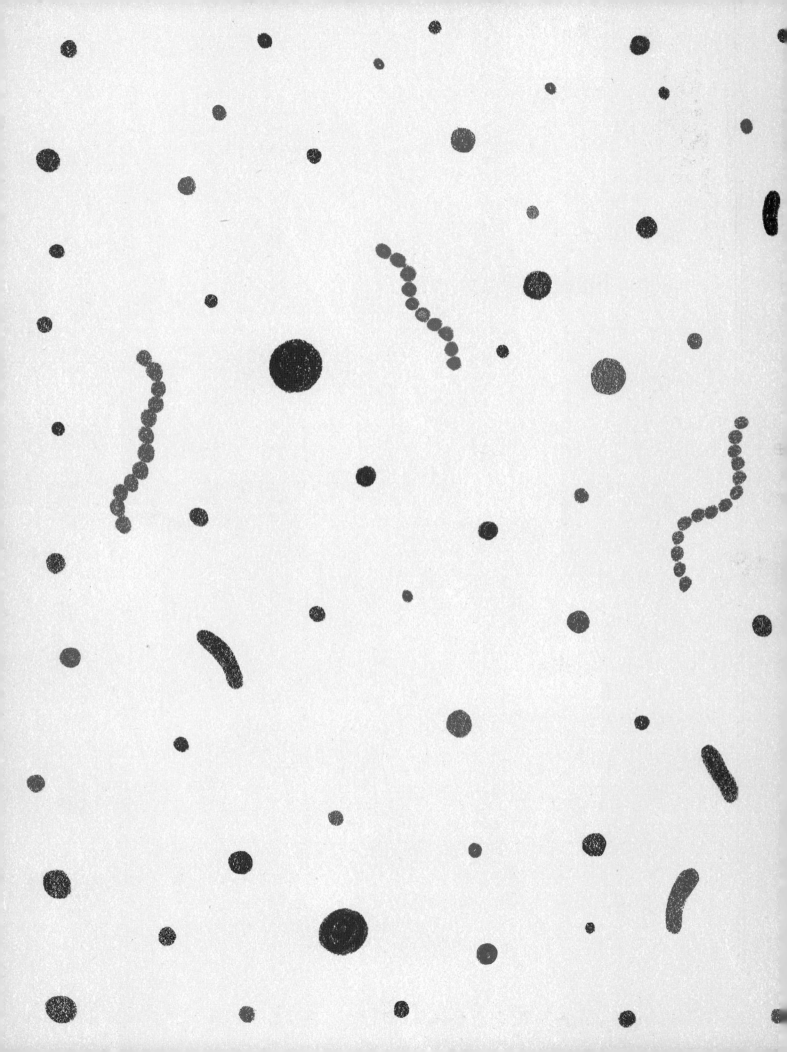